North American Indians Today

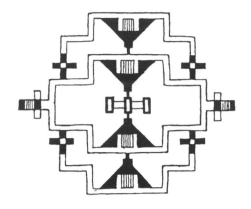

North American Indians Today

Apache

Cherokee

Cheyenne

Comanche

Creek

Crow

Huron

Iroquois

Navajo

Ojibwa

Osage

Potawatomi

Pueblo

Seminole

Sioux

North American
Indians Today

Cheyenne

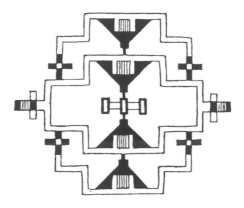

by
Kenneth McIntosh
and
Marsha McIntosh

Mason Crest Publishers

Philadelphia

We wish to thank all the wonderful people who helped us with this book, including Dr. Richard Littlebear, Conrad Fisher, Glenn Littlebird Jr., Leroy White Man, Elliot White Dirt, Dorothy Glenmore, the folks at Fort Laramie National Historical Site and St. Labre Mission School, Micaiah Birdinground, Reasco Killsnight, Warren Spang, Rick Robinson, Joseph Fire Crow, Gary Small, Pastor Willis Busenitz, Jessica Andrews, and the people at South Dakota Game, Fish, and Parks.

Mason Crest Publishers Inc.
370 Reed Road
Broomall, Pennsylvania 19008
(866) MCP-BOOK (toll free)

First printing
1 2 3 4 5 6 7 8 9 10
Library of Congress Cataloging-in-Publication Data on file at the Library of Congress.
ISBN: 1-59084-666-4
1-59084-663X (series)

Design by Lori Holland.
Composition by Bytheway Publishing Services, Binghamton, New York.
Cover design by Benjamin Stewart.
Printed in the Hashemite Kingdom of Jordan.
Photographs by Benjamin Stewart. Photos on pp. 18, 48 courtesy of Northwestern University Library; photos on p. 74 and the cover are courtesy of Senator Ben Nighthorse Campbell; photo on p. 70 courtesy of Joseph Fire Crow; photo on p. 23 courtesy of Ft. Laramie Historical Association; photo on p. 60 courtesy of the Smithsonian Museum of the American Indian; photos on pp. 59, 82 courtesy of Viola Ruelke Gommer. Drawings on pp. 6, 41 by Keith Rosko.

Contents

Why is it so important that Indians be brought into the "mainstream" of American life?
I would not know how to interpret this phrase to my people.
The closest I would be able to come would be "a big wide river".
Am I then to tell my people that they are to be thrown into the big, wide river of the United States?

Earl Old Person
Blackfeet Tribal Chairman

Introduction

In the midst of twenty-first-century North America, how do the very first North Americans hold on to their unique cultural identity? At the same time, how do they adjust to the real demands of the modern world? Earl Old Person's quote on the opposite page expresses the difficulty of achieving this balance. Even the common values of the rest of North America—like fitting into the "mainstream"—may seem strange or undesireable to North American Indians. How can these groups of people thrive and prosper in the twenty-first century without losing their traditions, the ways of thinking and living that have been handed down to them by their ancestors? How can they keep from drowning in North America's "big, wide river"?

Thoughts from the Series Consultant

Each of the books in this series was written with the help of Native scholars and tribal leaders from the particular tribe. Based on oral histories as well as written documents, these books describe the current strategies of each Native nation to develop its economy while maintaining strong ties with its culture. As a result, you may find that these books read far differently from other books about Native Americans.

Over the past centuries, Native groups have faced increasing pressure to conform to the wishes of the governments that took their lands. Often brutally inhumane methods were implemented to change Native social systems. These books describe the ways that Native groups refused to be passive recipients of change, even in the face of these past atrocities. Heroic individuals worked to fit external changes into local conditions. This struggle continues today.

The legacy of the past still haunts the psyche of both Native and non-Native people of North America; hopefully, these books will help correct some misunderstandings. And even with the difficulties encountered by past and current Native leaders, Native nations continue to thrive. As this series illustrates, Native populations continue to increase—and they have clearly persevered against incredible odds. North American culture's big, wide river may be deep and cold—but Native Americans are good swimmers!

—*Martha McCollough*

Breaking Stereotypes

One way that some North Americans may "drown" Native culture is by using stereotypes to think about North American Indians. When we use stereotypes to think about a group of people, we assume things about them because of their race or cultural group. Instead of taking time to understand individual differences and situations, we lump together everyone in a certain group. In reality, though, every person is different. More than two million Native people live in North America, and they are as **diverse** as any other group. Each one is unique.

Even if we try hard to avoid stereotypes, however, it isn't always easy to know what words to use. Should we call the people who are native to North America Native Americans—or American Indians—or just Indians?

The word "Indian" probably comes from a mistake—when Christopher Columbus arrived in the New World, he thought he had reached India, so he called the people he found there Indians. Some people feel it doesn't make much sense to call Native Americans "Indians." (Suppose Columbus had thought he landed in China instead of India; would we today call Native people "Chinese"?) Other scholars disagree; for example, Russell Means, Native politician and activist, claims that the word "Indian" comes from Columbus saying the native people were *en Dios*—"in God," or naturally spiritual.

Many Canadians use the term "First Nations" to refer to the Native peoples who live there, and people in the United States usually speak of Native Americans. Most Native people we talked to while we were writing these books prefer the simple term "Indian"—or they would rather use the names of their tribes. (We have used the term "North American Indians" for our series to distinguish this group of people from the inhabitants of India.)

Even the definition of what makes a person "Indian" varies. The U.S. government recognizes certain groups as tribal nations (almost 500 in all). Each nation then decides how it will enroll people as members of that tribe. Tribes may require a particular amount of Indian blood, tribal membership of the father or the mother, or other *criteria*. Some enrolled tribal members who are legally "Indian" may not look Native at all; many have blond hair and blue eyes and others have clearly African features. At the same time, there are thousands of Native people whose tribes have not yet been officially recognized by the government.

We have done our best to write books that are as free from stereotypes as possible. But you as the reader also play a part. After reading one of these books, we hope you won't think: "The Cheyenne are all like this" or "Iroquois are all like that." Each person in this world is unique, whatever their culture. Stereotypes shut people's minds—but these books are intended to open your mind. North American Indians today have much wisdom and beauty to offer.

Some people consider American Indians to be a historical topic only, but Indians today are living, contributing members of North American society. The contributions of the various Indian cultures enrich our world—and North America would be a very different place without the Native people who live there. May they never be lost in North America's "big, wide river"!

Before horses, bison were hunted by careful stalking or by stampeding them over cliffs.

Chapter 1

Sweet Medicine, Founder of the Cheyenne Way of Life

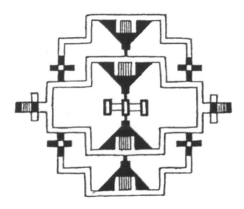

"Haaahe."
(greeting expression used by Cheyenne men)

People always need a hero. For North Americans today, that hero might be someone like Martin Luther King Jr. or Mother Teresa. For centuries, Native people in our country have had their own heroes to whom they looked for inspiration. These were people who lived long ago; the stories of their lives were told from generation to generation. For the Cheyenne, Sweet Medicine was such a hero.

At one time people had no laws; they barely knew how to survive, so they did shameful things, without even realizing it. One man, though, lived right. He and his family had a sense of honor.

One night the teenage daughter of this honorable man heard a man speak to her in a dream. "You are beautiful, yet you live right. Therefore Sweet Root will visit you."

The girl thought the voice was just a dream—but she kept having the same dream, and each time she dreamed, the voice seemed more real. She told her mother, "Something supernatural must be happening—the voice is so much like a man's voice."

"No," her mother denied, "it's just a dream."

But the daughter knew something strange and wonderful was happening. In a few months, she was obviously pregnant—and yet she insisted she had never had sex. Her parents believed her, but no one else did, so she went into hiding.

When her time came to give birth, she went out into the wilderness. There, all alone, she gave birth to a baby boy. In those wicked times, a boy without a father would be badly treated, so she dared not bring him back to her community. She dried the baby, wrapped him in soft moss, and left him alone in the wilderness. Praying someone would find him, she returned home crying.

An old woman was out looking for wild turnips when she heard the baby. She was overjoyed to find him, for she had never been able to have children of her own. All around the baby grew the sweet root that makes a mother's milk flow, so she named the boy Sweet Medicine and adopted him as her own.

Sweet Medicine grew faster and learned more than other boys. When he was only ten years old, he already had grown-up wisdom and hunting skills. But because his adopted family was poor, no one paid any attention to him.

That year a famine struck the village. "Grandmother," he said, "find me a worn-out buffalo hide."

The old woman found a hide that the starving dogs had been chewing on. When she showed it to Sweet Medicine, he told her, "Clean it in the river."

Then Sweet Medicine took a willow wand and bent it into a hoop. He cut the buffalo hide into string and wove it back and forth over the hoop,

Bison or Buffalo?

When North American Indians speak of the buffalo, technically they are referring to what scientists call the bison. "True" buffalo live in Asia and Africa, and they belong to a different family than the North American bison.

English settlers are thought to have been the first to use the word "buffalo" for the bison. French explorers called these large, shaggy animals *les boeufs*, the French word for oxen or cattle. The word evolved in English to variations such as "buffler," "boeffle," and "buffalo." Today, most North Americans use "bison" and "buffalo" interchangeably.

There are two types of North American bison:

1. Plains bison, with long beards and shaggy horns, are found in Texas and the Great Plains.
2. The wood bison, larger and darker than its southern cousin, is found in Canada and the northern United States.

making a kind of net. Then he made four sharp sticks. He said: "Grandmother, we're going to play the hoop-and-stick game. Roll this hoop for me."

She rolled the hoop along the ground and Sweet Medicine hurled his pointed sticks through the center of it, hitting the right spot every time. A crowd gathered to see the new game. Sweet Medicine threw his stick through the hoop—and the hoop turned into a buffalo calf! Instantly, it fell down dead; Sweet Medicine's stick had gone right through its heart.

The people were able to eat their fill, and that was the end of the famine. That's also how the Cheyenne got the stick-and-hoop game. This sacred game has much power attached to it, and it is still being played by the Cheyenne.

After Sweet Medicine killed his first buffalo, a rude and selfish older chief came up to him. "This is just the kind of hide I have been looking for," said the man. "I will take it."

"You can't have it," said Sweet Medicine. "It is my first kill." (The first

Members of the Northern Cheyenne tribe still receive spiritual guidance at places like Montana's Medicine Rock.

animal a boy kills is very important to the Cheyenne.) Sweet Medicine continued: "But you are welcome to half the meat, because I honor old age."

The chief grabbed the bison, and so did Sweet Medicine. Then the older man whipped Sweet Medicine with his riding crop. When he struck Sweet Medicine's face, the boy became angry. He grabbed a leg bone from the bison and hit the chief over the head. The chief fell down stunned.

The evil villagers were incensed. Some said, "Let's whip him"; others said, "Let's kill him."

Sweet Medicine said to his grandmother, "Some young men of the warrior societies will come here to kill me for having stood up for myself." He thanked her for her kindness to him, and then fled from the village. When the young warriors came, they were so angry to find the boy gone that they pulled down the old woman's lodge and set fire to it.

The boy wandered the prairie alone. One day he heard a voice calling. It led him to a mountain shaped like a huge tepee—the sacred mountain called Bear Butte. Sweet Medicine found a secret opening and entered the mountain. It was hollow inside and filled with powerful spirits.

"Grandson, come in, we have been expecting you," the holy people said. These spirit people then taught Sweet Medicine the Cheyenne way to live so that he could return to the people and teach them.

The holy people gave Sweet Medicine sacred objects that would enable the people to prosper. They taught him wise laws. They taught him how women should be honored. They taught him the many useful things people had not yet learned at that time. Finally, they taught him how to make a sacred tepee in which the arrows were to be kept. An old spirit man burned sweet grass to purify both Sweet Medicine and the sacred arrow bundle. Then the Cheyenne boy put the holy bundle on his back and began the long journey home to his people.

During his absence, another famine had stricken the land, and the people were starving. Sweet Medicine met some children whose ribs were sticking out from hunger. They were making mud toys shaped like buffalo. Sweet Medicine turned their toys into buffalo meat and told the boys to go home and tell the village he was returning.

Two young hunters came out of the town to find Sweet Medicine. He told them: "I have come bringing a wonderful gift from the Creator that the spirits inside the great medicine mountain have sent you. Set up a big lodge in the center of the camp circle. Cover its floor with *sage*, and purify it. Tell everyone to go inside the tepee and stay there."

When this was done, Sweet Medicine walked toward the village and called out four times: "People of the Cheyenne, with a great power I am approaching. Be joyful. I am bringing sacred objects." He entered the big lodge and said, "You have not yet learned the right way to live. That is why the ones above were angry and the buffalo went into hiding."

Sweet Medicine filled a deer-bone pipe with sacred tobacco. All night, he taught the people what the spirits had taught him. These teachings established the way of the Cheyenne nation. When he had finished teaching, Sweet Medicine sang four sacred songs. After each song he smoked the pipe, and its smoke arose as prayers to the Great Mystery.

When people left the sacred tepee, they found the prairie around them covered with buffalo. The spirits were no longer angry. The famine was over. From then on, the people followed the laws the spirits had given Sweet Medicine—the Cheyenne way of life. As long as the people obeyed these laws, they prospered.

The Creator gave Sweet Medicine four times the length of a normal life, but even Sweet Medicine was not immortal. (Only the rocks and the mountains are forever.) When he grew old and knew death was near, he asked the people to carry him to a place near the sacred Bear Butte. They set up a lodge there for him to rest in. Then, he addressed the people for the last time:

Pictographs at Medicine Rock portray traditions sacred to the Northern Cheyenne.

Sweet Medicine's prophetic words emphasize the value of women for the people's survival. This museum display shows the traditional dress for Cheyenne women.

I have seen in a vision that some day, long after I am gone, light-skinned bearded men will arrive with sticks spitting fire. They will conquer the land and drive you before them. They will kill the animals who give you their flesh that you may live, and they will bring strange animals for you to ride and eat. They will introduce war and evil, strange sickness and death. They will try and make you forget the Creator and the things I have taught you. They will impose their own alien, evil ways. They will take your land little by little until there is nothing left for you. I do not like to tell you this, but you must know. You must be strong when that bad time comes, you men, and particularly you women, because much depends on you, because you are the perpetuators of life and if you weaken, the Cheyenne will cease to be. Now I have said all there is to say.

Those were Sweet Medicine's last words. The Cheyenne are still strong today. Because he taught his people the right way to live, Sweet Medicine was the truest kind of hero.

When Edward Curtis took this picture in 1927, the traditional way of living had been gone for decades. Curtis would sometimes provide war bonnets or buckskin clothing for his subjects, to create a more "romantic" image of the Indian.

Chapter 2

Survivors of Genocide on the Great Plains

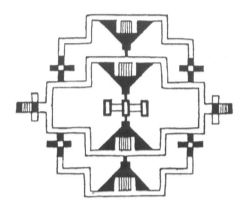

"Those are two fifty-caliber bullet holes in that little girl's head." An angry Northern Cheyenne man pointed to a box that held the skull of a three-year-old child. "Put that in the newspaper," he told a reporter.

Both the reporter and the Northern Cheyenne man were at an unusual and emotional burial service on a cold, rainy day in Busby, Montana. On October 16, 1993, a small crowd, mostly Northern Cheyenne, had gathered to see eighteen murder victims buried in their native land.

These were the remains of Cheyenne men, women, and children belonging to Chief Dull Knife's band. They had died more than a hundred years ago in an incredible effort to reach their ancestral home after they had escaped from a death camp at Fort Robinson, Nebraska. Their story was just one sad chapter in the saga of the Northern Cheyenne and their valiant efforts to live as they chose.

Today, there are more than seven thousand Northern Cheyenne. "Cheyenne" is not their own name for themselves; it comes from a Sioux Indian word meaning "Little Cree." Their *traditional* name is "Tsetsêhesêstâhase," which means "we people." Most live on the Northern Cheyenne Reservation, which covers 444,000 acres (approximately 180,000 hectares) in Southern Montana.

Originally, the Tsetsêhesêstâhase dwelt in Minnesota. They lived by fishing, catching small game, and gathering wild foods. Neighboring tribes acquired guns from traders and forced the Tsetsêhesêstâhase out of these lands. They moved to the short grass prairies of North Dakota. There, they lived in large earth lodges and grew corn, beans, squash, and other crops.

In the early 1700s, they met a group named the Sutaio. At first the Cheyenne thought they would have to fight with the Sutaio. Warriors of the two tribes lined up facing one another and called out challenges. Both groups were astonished that they could understand one another. Seeing that their languages were so similar, they became friends. Eventually the Sutaio joined with the Cheyenne.

Memorial for a Massacre

A U.S. Congressman and a casino owner are working to make a memorial to one of America's darkest misdeeds. Senator Ben Nighthorse Campbell, a Northern Cheyenne related to victims of the 1864 Sand Creek Massacre, sponsored a plan to create a memorial on the site. The site will consist of approximately 12,480 acres (approximately 5,053 hectares) in Kiowa County, Colorado, the site of the Sand Creek Massacre. The owner of a ranch at the scene of the massacre wanted $1.5 million for the property. The owner of an Indian casino in Oklahoma bought the land for the Cheyenne. The future memorial will ensure that hundreds of Cheyenne who died at Sand Creek are never forgotten.

Before they met any Europeans, the Cheyenne and other tribes had many horses, which had escaped from the Spanish.

In the late 1700s, the Tsetsèhesèstáhase changed their way of living yet again. They had obtained horses that had escaped from the Spanish, and on horseback, they could hunt the great bison more easily. Horses replaced dogs as beasts of burden, and the Tsetsèhesèstáhase soon had great herds of horses. They had to keep moving their villages, since the horses would eat all the grass around their camps.

At this time, the Cheyenne consisted of ten major bands. The Council of Forty-four Chiefs helped the bands communicate with each other. Some bands roamed southward seeking to gain horses and trade buffalo hides.

The Cheyenne traded and fought with neighboring Indian nations. The greatest honor in battle was to touch an enemy with a curved stick—without killing him. This perilous feat was called "counting coup." Warrior societies, such as the legendary Dog Soldiers, fought especially dangerous missions.

Bison provided the necessities of life for the Native people of the plains. White hunters drove the buffalo almost to extinction in the 1880s. This painting is by Leroy White Man, a Cheyenne artist.

Bison provided the necessities of life. A single bull might weigh over two thousand pounds, and since there were millions of buffalo in Montana alone, the Cheyenne experienced no shortage of food.

Cheyenne chiefs were noted for generosity, even to enemies. Chief Highbacked Wolf, for example, once came upon a badly injured Pawnee warrior alone on the prairie. The Cheyenne were at war with the Pawnee, but Highbacked Wolf announced to his startled enemy: "Here are clothes, and I have three horses—you may choose one."

Cheyenne women were noted for their modesty. They also **abstained** from sex before marriage. Seeing their way of life, one frontiersman reported, "They live in constant exercise of moral and Christian virtues, though they know it not."

The **Oregon Trail** ran between the northern and southern bands of the Cheyenne, separating them. The Fort Wise Treaty of 1861 established a reservation for the southern bands. Today, the Southern Cheyenne live in Oklahoma.

In 1851, an immense gathering of Indian tribes met at Fort Laramie to sign treaties with the United States. The government promised traditional hunting grounds to both Northern and Southern Cheyenne in exchange for the right to build forts and trade on their lands. The treaty was a bad deal for the Cheyenne. In 1853, some 15,000 whites passed through Cheyenne land, slaughtering herds of buffalo, spreading devastating diseases, and treating Indians with contempt. Both the Northern and Southern Cheyenne tribes decided they would fight to keep their lands. A series of skirmishes took place between Cheyenne warriors and U.S. soldiers.

On the morning of November 29, 1864, hundreds of Southern Cheyenne were sleeping at their encampment on the shores of Sand Creek, Colorado.

Fort Laramie was the site of the first treaty between the Northern Cheyenne and the U.S. Government. The treaty was promptly broken as the government allowed large numbers of non-Indians onto Indian lands.

Medicine Rock is a sacred site. It has been marked with pictographs, such as those on the next page.

They had been invited to a nearby fort to sign a peace treaty, but instead, more than a thousand soldiers, commanded by Colonel John Chivington, attacked the unsuspecting Cheyenne. With both hands raised in a sign of surrender and holding an American flag, Chief White Antelope walked toward the soldiers. He was shot down.

Four hunded Indians were slaughtered. Women and children were shot dead at point blank range or beaten to death. The white soldier cut off their victims' sexual organs for keepsakes. Later, when asked to explain his actions, Chivington told a gathering of ministers, "It is simply not possible for Indians to obey or even understand any treaty. To kill them is the only way for peace in Colorado." Grateful settlers named a town after Colonel Chivington. The Indians were promised payment for this **atrocity**, but they never received it.

Black Kettle's band of Cheyenne had been at Sand Creek. Almost four years to the day after the massacre, the survivors of this band were again resting in their tepees, just as they had been before Chivington's attack. This time the Cheyenne were encamped along the Washita River—and once again, soldiers attacked and butchered men, women, and children.

The commander was General George Armstrong Custer. Despite terrible defeats like this, however, the Northern Cheyenne continued to fight for their lands.

On June 25, 1876, thousands of Lakota and Cheyenne had come together, forming an enormous camp. They were enjoying a beautiful summer afternoon on the Little Bighorn River when Seventh Cavalry troops led by Major Reno rode into the camp, firing at every Indian they saw. Native warriors grabbed their weapons and defended their village.

General Custer and his troops came in on the other side of the camp. His last reported words were, "We've caught them napping, boys!" He soon found himself surrounded. Lame White Man, a Northern Cheyenne warrior, led a charge that broke the soldiers' defenses—and died doing so. Less than an hour later, Custer and all his men were dead. Many shot themselves rather than face the shame of defeat at the hands of the Cheyenne and Lakota.

This pictograph is at Medicine Rock. In 1876, Cheyenne and Sioux held a Sun Dance at this place. Sioux Chief Sitting Bull received a vision of soldiers falling into the camp. This vision was fulfilled on June 25, when the Seventh Cavalry was defeated after charging into the tribes' encampment.

Markers at Little Bighorn Battlefield commemorate the soldiers under General Custer's command who died there. On June 25, 2003, a new memorial was dedicated at the site to the Sioux and Cheyenne Indians who died in the battle.

Among the many Northern Cheyenne who fought bravely in this battle were Wooden Leg, Yellow Nose, White Bull, John Sun Bear, and Brave Wolf. Brave Bear counted coup on one of Reno's men and later was in the thick of battle near General Custer. Buffalo Calf Road Woman fought beside her husband, Black Coyote, throughout the battle. She was later renamed Brave Woman. A hundred Lakota and Cheyenne died in the battle along with 268 soldiers.

Little Bighorn was a notable victory for the Northern Cheyenne and Lakota. Unfortunately, sensational coverage of the battle in Eastern papers created a public outcry against the Plains Indians. Massive numbers of troops were sent to conquer them.

The Northern Cheyenne could not fight forever. In 1877, they surrendered. The government forced the tribe to walk to Oklahoma and join the Southern Cheyenne.

Conditions in Oklahoma were terrible. The Cheyenne could not produce enough food to live. Diseases swept through their camps. In one year, fifty-eight of the Northern Cheyenne died.

In 1878, Northern Cheyenne Chief Dull Knife announced to the agent in charge of the reserve; "I am going north to my own country. I do not want to see blood spilt about this agency. Let me get a little distance away. Then if you want to fight, I will fight you, and we can make the ground bloody at that place."

Three hundred fifty-three Northern Cheyenne followed Dull Knife and another chief, Little Wolf, off the reservation. They outmaneuvered and outfought thousands of soldiers all the way to northern Nebraska. There, Dull Knife and Little Wolf separated into two groups.

Dull Knife's band were captured and taken to Fort Robinson. The government ordered them returned to Oklahoma, but they refused to be moved. American troops locked the men in a large building and denied them food and water. The band's women sneaked weapons to them, though, and on January 9, 1879, Dull Knife's people broke out of Fort Robinson.

Some were killed escaping; others ran into the frozen hills. A week later, the army caught and slaughtered a number of families. Their bodies were

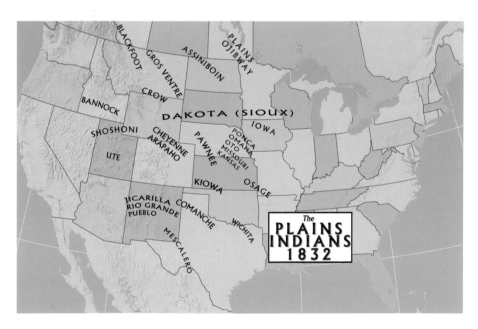

A map of Indian tribes' territories in 1832 shows the enormous scope of the Cheyenne before miners, settlers, and soldiers invaded their lands.

dumped in a pit, their skulls sent to Washington for exhibition. These were the remains returned to their people in 1993.

Dull Knife and a few others escaped to join friends at the Lakota reservation. Little Wolf's band fared better. They hid for the winter and eventually moved into the Lame Deer, Montana, area. On November 26, 1884, the government finally gave the Northern Cheyenne their own reservation.

Now, they faced a new sort of threat; their lives were no longer attacked, but their culture was. Government policy at this time favored assimilation; that is, Indians were supposed to blend in with white culture. The Indian Agency boarding schools were powerful tools for assimilation. The philosophy of many of these schools was: "Kill the Indian to save the child." Students were forced to wear white people's clothes and follow white customs. They were punished for speaking their native language or practicing traditional ways. Disease killed many Indian children in the dormitories. An exception to these practices was a school run by Mennonite missionaries. Students there were encouraged to speak and read in their native language. On the reservation, however, the U.S. government punished traditional ways of worship.

Early in the 1900s, the Northern Cheyenne began to experience some prosperity as they learned to raise cattle. Expert horsemen, they made fine

A carved horse head by Northern Cheyenne artist Leroy White Man reflects his personal love for horses.

Peace pipes are still important ceremonial objects to many Native people. The stem and bowl are kept separated, in special bags, until actual use. Smoke is a form of prayer. Indians in the old days never smoked hallucinogenic drugs, contrary to some Hollywood depictions. Doing so would profane the pipe.

War bonnets like this were seldom worn in actual battles. Instead, they were symbols of achievement, like medals worn today by veterans on parade.

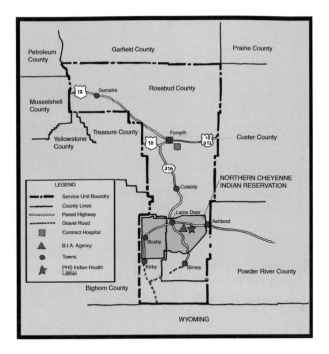

The Northern Cheyenne Nation today. Dull Knife, Little Wolf, and their followers struggled against incredible odds to reclaim these lands.

cowboys. In 1914, the government stepped in again, though, and ordered that the Northern Cheyenne could only have one herd on the reservation. This didn't work well, and bitter winters in 1919 and 1920 killed almost all their cattle.

In 1919, the U.S. government dealt the Northern Cheyenne yet another blow. The government said the Northern Cheyenne would have to kill their horses to provide adequate feed for the cattle. The Tsetsėhesėstȧhase refused to do this. They considered their horses to be practically family. So the government stepped in and slaughtered the horses—and then fed the meat to the tribe. Some horses were sold, without a penny going to their owners.

In the 1920s, a new government policy called allotment threatened to break up the Northern Cheyenne nation. This plan divided up reservation land between individuals. Each person could sell his or her plot of land if they wished to. Most of the Indians were poor, and this policy was designed to encourage richer non-Indians to buy out the Cheyenne's land. But the Northern Cheyenne, having fought so desperately for this place,

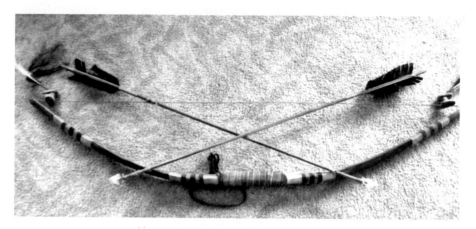

Leroy White Man still has the bow and arrows belonging to one of his ancestors. The bow and arrow could be reloaded on horseback more easily than firearms, until repeating guns were invented at the time of the Civil War. A well-placed arrow could bring down even the largest bison.

Chief Dull Knife College is named after the man who led his people on an incredible, death-defying march from the horrible conditions on an Oklahoma reservation back to their homeland.

refused to sell. Their united determination to keep their land has helped them maintain their identity.

The following decades brought some gains and some losses for the Northern Cheyenne Nation. In 1934, John Collier, President Franklin D. Roosevelt's Chief of Indian Affairs, established the Indian Reorganization Act. This was called the "Indian New Deal." Tribes were recognized as *sovereign nations*, entitled to handle their economics and manage their own lands. At this time, the Northern Cheyenne adopted a written tribal *constitution*.

One good result of the Indian New Deal was the encouragement of traditional Indian worship. The Sun Dance and other important traditions were allowed once again.

Following World War II, the Northern Cheyenne faced another attempt to do away with their lands when the U.S. government tried to merge the Northern Cheyenne with the American Indians on the Crow Reservation. The Northern Cheyenne and Crow were traditional enemies, and this did not go over well with either group.

In the 1970s, the tribe made new efforts to preserve their language and culture. For example, the Council of Forty-four Chiefs was restored. In 1973, both Southern and Northern Cheyenne met to coordinate traditional chiefs and warrior societies.

At the same time, the Northern Cheyenne encountered a new sort of threat. Coal companies bought exploratory *permits* to Northern Cheyenne land. These permits included the option for companies to lease the land they were exploring. People on the reservation soon realized the majority of their land could be turned into *strip mines*. The tribe began a number of lawsuits designed to cancel the leases.

An important part of the battle against coal was the Northern Cheyenne Research Project. This was an environmental study of air, water, land, and wildlife on the reservation. The Northern Cheyenne told the Environmental Protection Agency they wanted air on the reservation to be "Class I." This means the air is free of pollution. Normally, only national parks and wilderness areas have air this clean. In 1978, legislation in the U.S. Congress was passed canceling the coal leases. Once again, the Northern Cheyenne had fought for their land and won.

Glenn Littlebird, Jr. served as a tribal councilman from 1998 through 2002.

Chapter 3

Current Government

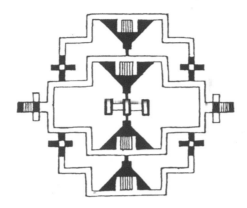

Her Indian name is Thunder and Lightning Woman. It sounds impressive, which is fitting for a woman of impressive accomplishments. In the year 2000, Geri Small was elected to be the first woman president of the Northern Cheyenne Reservation. She is the only female president leading a tribe in Montana or Wyoming.

But she is not the first woman to lead a Cheyenne tribe. In the 1800s, there was a Cheyenne leader named North Woman. Her people called her North Woman because she gave them direction (just as the North Star gives direction to travelers) and because she helped lead them north from Oklahoma to Montana, the tribe's ancestral land. Cheyenne traditions say this *medicine woman* led her people home through a net of soldiers, relying on supernatural visions to outmaneuver her foes. In this century, however, the Northern Cheyenne have had few strong women leaders—until Geri Small.

Geri's sister Gail is another sort of leader, one who has been active in environmental issues for years. Gail describes what Geri is doing as reservation president:

> Geri is trying to rebuild the entire reservation water system. She's trying to rebuild the roads and the *infrastructure*. These aren't sexy issues. These aren't battles with the government over sovereignty or Indian rights. This is grunt work, the work in the trenches. We're rebuilding a nation from the ground up.

The U.S. Department of the Interior must officially recognize each Indian tribe in order for them to be granted status as a sovereign nation. At present, the government recognizes 556 tribes—and the Northern Cheyenne are among them. As a sovereign nation, the Northern Cheyenne have the right to make and enforce their own laws, elect their own leadership, and negotiate as a nation with the United States. They cannot, however, take any actions that would undermine the laws or welfare of the U.S. federal government.

Today's Northern Cheyenne tribal government was formed in the 1930s in response to the U.S. government's Indian Reorganization Act. Like the Ameri-

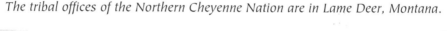

The tribal offices of the Northern Cheyenne Nation are in Lame Deer, Montana.

Northern Cheyenne tribal council chambers.

can government, the tribal government has three branches: executive, legislative, and judicial. The executive branch includes the president, vice president, treasurer, and secretary. These officers are responsible for all tribal programs. The legislative department consists of the judges and a ***probation officer***.

The council is elected every two years, but the members serve for four years; they have staggered terms so the whole council is not all new every election year. The president is elected every four years. The council appoints members for boards and committees. Unlike the U.S. federal government, the council has no regular speaker of the house. Instead, one of the strongest leaders is usually called on to lead.

Tribal councils today have great power and responsibility in their communities. They protect the land and water rights of the tribe. They negotiate with other governments. They make laws for the tribe. They watch over businesses and charitable organizations. In short, they are involved in almost every major matter within tribal borders.

Glenn Littlebird, Jr. is one member of the Northern Cheyenne Nation who has experienced firsthand the power of the tribal council. He served as tribal councilman from 1998 through 2002.

The Bureau of Indian Affairs Offices on the Northern Cheyenne Reservation.

Glenn grew up on the reservation, but as an adult, he moved away for a number of years and worked for the **Bureau of Indian Affairs** (BIA) as a criminal investigator. He also worked in law enforcement. In 1996, he came home to live on the Northern Cheyenne Reservation, where he was elected as tribal judge and later as a council member.

One of the council's duties is to bring in funding for needed programs. Glenn went to Albuquerque to talk with one of the BIA leaders. He let the man know how badly his people needed funding for better communications on the reservation. They had no cell phone capability—which meant if police were chasing an offender, they couldn't phone for backup. The police also needed new cars. The BIA listened to Glenn's requests, and the tribe was given grant money for these needs.

The tribe is now building the Northern Cheyenne Youth Services Center in Busby, Montana, with funding provided by the BIA. This will be a juvenile detention hall, which will also employ forty people. Tribal court will also be held there. Since the tribe is hoping to intervene early in the lives of juvenile offenders so they won't graduate to hard crime, the Youth Services

Center will also provide traditional healing and guidance for at-risk teens. That is something Indian teens don't get in non-Indian detention and counseling facilities.

The tribal council also works to bring economic development to the reservation. A recent product of their efforts is the tribal casino. Fifty percent of its profits go to the tribe. In 2001, the tribe received $80,000 from the casino, which was spent on programs for elders, education, and youth. Currently, the council is working on a mushroom farm project as well. The council hopes to build a 10,000-square-foot (930-square-meter) building for this purpose. The mushrooms would be sold to grocery stores, providing more jobs for workers on the reservation. The council also has plans to renovate a gas station in Ashland, turning it into a truck stop complete with showers and lounge.

The Tribal Employment Rights Office is in charge of transportation on the Northern Cheyenne Reservation. This office is working on paving all the roads on the reservation. Main roads are paved now, but not all the side roads.

Tribal government is not only responsible for business transactions within its own nation; it also handles business with the state and federal governments. A recent important issue was Otter Creek coal development.

Northern Cheyenne Tribal Health Offices.

Northern Cheyenne Tribal Court House, Lame Deer, Montana.

Women's Role

"Every ceremony has a role for women, but not every role is the woman's. I'm very respectful of my role as a Cheyenne woman, but that doesn't mean I can't be president of my tribe."

—Geri Small

A nation is not conquered until the hearts of its women are on the ground.

Then it is done...

No matter how brave its warriors, nor how strong its weapons.

-traditional Cheyenne saying

The State of Montana owns land near Yellowstone National Park and wanted to receive money for coal mining there. The U.S. government was concerned that coal development would harm wildlife in the national park, so the federal government and Montana exchanged lands. The coal mining development ended up in the Otter Creek area, just three miles outside the Northern Cheyenne Reservation.

The Northern Cheyenne hired an attorney and approached the state

Bureau of Indian Affairs Tribal Law Enforcement headquarters on the Northern Cheyenne Reservation.

with an offer. They would drop a lawsuit against the Interior Department that had held up transfer of federal coal land to the state since 1996. In exchange for dropping that lawsuit, the state would make a law that Indians who live within fifty miles of Otter Creek must be hired before other workers to work in the coal mines. This will give the Northern Cheyenne needed jobs.

The governor of Montana, however, opposed the Northern Cheyenne's demand for priority in hiring. The coal developers also opposed the deal. Nevertheless, the state land board granted the Northern Cheyenne's request. Steve Chestnut, an attorney for the Northern Cheyenne, explained the reasoning behind the tribe's actions: "Industry does not do the kinds of things we're asking for voluntarily, out of the goodness of their heart." When tribal president Geri Small presented her people's case before the state land board, she commented, "Our ancestors resided in Otter Creek and many of our ancestors are buried there."

Many years have passed from the days of North Woman, who struggled to bring her people back to Montana, to tribal president Geri Small, who fights legal battles to help her people get jobs. One thing hasn't changed: the Northern Cheyenne still need strong leaders who will point the way for their people and protect them against outside threats.

The spiritual growth Clayton Small experienced on the reservation led him to work on a Ph.D. *dissertation* about healing and recovery for Indian men. While working on his degree in Spokane, Washington, he met with other Native professional men, and they decided to form a group. He told Simonelli:

> I built a sweat lodge on my property and the men would come for dinner. We would pray together and cry and laugh together. It was powerful making that connection knowing that there were other men who are in the same boat, who are struggling with the same issues. And we helped each other grow.

Clayton Small eventually developed the "Good Road of Life Model" for Native men's groups. Groups address alcoholism and other addictions, multigenerational trauma and cultural oppression, father/son relationships, spirituality, and role modeling and service to the community. Small says, "The core or essence of the Good Road of Life Model is the incorporation of Native spirituality. Spirituality is the driving force that allows Native men to not only seek a new beginning, but to continue the healing journey."

Today's Cheyenne worship in a variety of ways. Many follow the ways of their ancestors, honoring the Creator, the earth, and their ancient ceremonies. Others belong to the Native American Church, a more recent spiritual practice shared by Indians across America. Others worship in traditional Christian ways, as Catholics or members of Protestant *denominations*.

Traditionally, the Cheyenne worship One Supreme Being, Ma'heo'o. Under Ma'heo'o, they revere four Sacred Persons who live at the four directions of the universe. Earth is revered as Grandmother and respected as a living being. As one Northern Cheyenne elder says:

> Our worldview and attitude toward nature is very different from that of the non-Indian. We see ourselves as part of nature, and we relate to it spiritually. Our people have always had deep reverence for land and nature. They felt intimate with it. Our white brother, however, does just the opposite, he tries to master nature.

Traditional Cheyenne religion calls on the sun, moon, thunder, and stars for blessings. All creation is regarded as living, and all of creation can

Sun Dance Not for Sale

Imitations of Northern Cheyenne Sun Dances are held in several places around the country. Reacting to this, Northern Cheyenne spiritual leaders have released a letter to the general public.

We, the Northern People who from time immemorial have practiced the traditional Sun Dance ways of our grandfathers and grandmothers, hereby conclude that the Sun Dance of the Northern Cheyenne is to remain on our Northern Cheyenne home-land. The Sun Dance is our lifeline and we will not play with nor sell nor bargain with any of its rites, related ceremonials, and songs.

Over the years, many Christian groups have established churches on the Northern Cheyenne Reservation.

impart the supernatural blessings of Ma'heo'o . . . if people are sensitive to spiritual reality.

According to Cheyenne belief, Ma'heo'o made sacred agreements with the Tsetsêhesêstâhase. The sweat ceremony is one way traditional Northern Cheyenne communicate with God. Prayers in the sweat lodge may be for loved ones, for those who are ill, or for power to face a challenge. Some people participate in sweat lodge ceremonies several times a year; some do daily.

The sweat lodge is built from a dome-shaped framework made from willow saplings. This is covered with blankets or skins and then blessed by a spiritual leader. During the sweat ceremony, water is poured over heated rocks, releasing hot steam into the lodge. The door is covered with a flap to keep the steam inside, and the interior's temperatures rise to over 200 degrees Fahrenheit (92.4 degrees Celsius). Spoken prayers are combined with prayers of cedar bark incense. The sweat ceremony is intensely spiritual, but it also has physical value, since the sweat removes *toxins* from the body.

The Sun Dance is another sacred ceremony, one that fulfills an age-old agreement with the Creator. Traditional warrior societies and Sun Dance

Edward Curtis photographed this Sun Dance lodge in 1927. Through much of the twentieth century, government officials who hoped to eradicate "superstition" prohibited the ceremony. The continuation of Cheyenne traditional belief is a credit to their faith and fortitude.

Many Native people use a sweat lodge like this one as their way of communicating with the Creator and purifying the body.

priests, who know the proper ways to behave and pray during the event, lead the dance. It is of great spiritual significance in the lives of those who have participated in it.

Recently, traditional Northern Cheyenne spiritual leaders have been troubled by non-Indians mimicking their traditions. For instance, non-Indians have attempted to perform sweat ceremonies without proper knowledge of how to do so. A few people have even died in non-Indian ceremonies, where the lodge lacked proper ventilation. A man in California was legally convicted of *fraud* for claiming to be a Cheyenne "shaman." He charged fees to talk about Indian traditions and conduct "sacred" ceremonies. In fact, however, he had no Indian blood—but he did have a long history of criminal charges.

The Northern Cheyenne are on guard against cultural invasions such as these. Traditional Northern Cheyenne have also taken action to preserve their sacred lands.

Bear Butte is located in western South Dakota on the edge of the Black Hills. It is now a state park, but Bear Butte is also the place where Sweet Medicine met the Spirit People and received the sacred teachings (see chapter one). The Northern Cheyenne go to this special place for prayer and to seek guidance. The following notice has been placed beside a trail at Bear Butte:

> A Religious Shrine—As Mount Sinai is to the Christians and Mecca is to the Moslems, Bear Butte is to the Plains Indians—a most sacred spiritual place. Many Indians today continue to have faith in the beliefs of natural power in the universe and they recognize the similarity between their Great Spirit and the God of the white man. As the different Christian groups each have their own church, many Indians feel they too are entitled to worship in their traditional ways. For many tribes Bear Butte is their church. Please respect the beliefs of the Indian people who visit the "wilderness" areas of this mountain to pray and fast. Stay on the marked trail and avoid the special ritual areas.

Along with distinct Northern Cheyenne beliefs, many members of the tribe have chosen to worship in the way offered by the Native American Church. The Native American Church is a "Pan-Indian" movement, which means that it combines the beliefs of many different North American Indian tribes. Although it is called a church, the Native American Church does not promote the beliefs of any particular Christian group. It combines traditional American Indian symbolism with Christian beliefs. The Native

Members of the Northern Cheyenne tribe leave prayer ribbons at sacred sites.

The church building at St. Labre Catholic Mission is shaped like a tepee. Symbols in the church are adapted from Cheyenne art and culture.

American Church uses peyote, a small, spineless cactus, as a **sacramental** substance, similar to the way wine is used in the Christian ritual of communion. The Native American Church teaches strict morality. Members must not drink alcohol, they must be faithful to their spouses, honest, and nonviolent.

The Catholic Church established St. Labre Mission on the reservation in 1884. The mission now has three educational centers that provide education to more than seven hundred Northern Cheyenne and Crow Indian children. The three campuses offer tuition-free education from preschool to twelfth grade. Courses in Northern Cheyenne language and culture are taught as well as general education. More than a thousand meals are served daily on the three campuses, and college scholarships are offered to help graduates.

The church building at St. Labre in Ashland is shaped like a tepee. A metal cross is the center lodge pole, and symbols in the church are adapted from Northern Cheyenne art and culture. The Stations of the Cross, which depict the events of Christ's crucifixion, are pecked into rock like the ancient **petroglyphs** near the reservation.

St. Labre Mission employs three hundred people; half the employees are Northern Cheyenne. The executive director of the schools, Curtis Yarlott, is a member of the nearby Crow Tribe, and a number of Crow children attend the school.

The mission has generated some **controversy**. Opponents criticize its fund-raising methods. Without a doubt, however, many Northern Cheyenne have benefited from the charitable and educational work of the mission.

Mennonite churches have also been on the Northern Cheyenne Reservation for nearly a century. (Mennonites are a Christian denomination that emphasizes charitable work and nonviolence.) Beginning in 1916, they encouraged the Northern Cheyenne to use their own language in church and school. The Mennonites have translated the Bible into Cheyenne.

Over the years, more Christian groups have come onto the Northern Cheyenne Reservation—Baptists, Mormons, Pentecostals, and Lutherans.

The first Catholic church was established on the Northern Cheyenne Reservation in 1884. There are now several.

A dancer portrayed on Medicine Rock attests to the ancient roots of spiritual beliefs that give strength to many of the Cheyenne today.

Some of these churches still expect their members to turn away from their Indian identity. Sometimes competition and dislike have strained the relationships between the churches. Despite these tensions, many Northern Cheyenne find spiritual strength and comfort in the Christian faith.

Faith takes different forms among the Northern Cheyenne. Some people pray in sweat lodges, others in churches. Some use peyote as a sacrament, others use bread and wine. Whatever the religious form, however, faith in the Creator gives spiritual strength to the Northern Cheyenne today.

Gilbert White Dirt is the Head Man of the Elk Horn Scrapers, who ensure that ceremonies are properly conducted.

Chapter 5

Social Structures Today

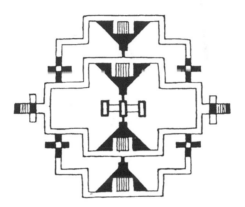

Gilbert White Dirt is an esteemed elder of the Northern Cheyenne tribe. His grandmother met Custer when she was twelve years old. With a family history deeply rooted in the past, Gilbert is also very much a part of the present.

He dances, sings, and performs in rodeos. Once, he even sang on Queen Elizabeth's yacht. Gilbert has also held the honored position of headman with the Elk Horn Scrapers, whose job it is to make sure the ceremonies of the tribe are performed correctly. Gilbert is concerned that the teens of his tribe seem less interested in learning the traditions of the elders than previous generations were.

Families have long been the strength of the Northern Cheyenne. Since the tepee days, extended families have shared homes. In Northern Chey-

Dorothy Glenmore is educational coordinator for the Head Start program in Lame Deer on the Northern Cheyenne Reservation.

enne tradition, first cousins are "brother" or "sister," and great-aunts are "Grandma" or "Grandpa." A non-Indian, getting acquainted with Northern Cheyenne people, often thinks, "They have big families!"

Traditional Northern Cheyenne values, such as honesty and generosity, are learned in the home. Today, if someone loses his job or home, or suffers some other misfortune, he can count on being taken in by a member of the family. If anyone has a real need, family members will raise money somehow to see that whatever he needs is provided.

In past centuries, parents and extended family taught culture and values. The home was the place where children learned their traditions and proper behavior. Now, schools and institutions outside the home are more responsible for teaching these things.

As the educational coordinator for the Head Start program in Lame Deer on the Northern Cheyenne Reservation, Dorothy Glenmore has a vital job. The reservation has eight Head Start centers, and each center serves twenty children. Sometimes special speakers come to the centers, people who may be dancers, artists, or elders. Recently, a tribal member came and talked about feathers. He taught the Cheyenne word for feather, and how to respect and care for these sacred objects.

The *mission statement* of Northern Cheyenne Head Start reads: "Treasure the past, nurture the present, transform the future." In order to do this, the Head Start centers are making a special effort to teach the Cheyenne language. One of the centers has a *language immersion* program where the children speak in Cheyenne throughout the day.

The Boys & Girls Club also has a role to play in the modern Northern Cheyenne social structure. The club helps Northern Cheyenne children and teens improve their lives. Rick J. Robinson is the director and founder of the club.

As a teenager, Rick got in trouble with alcohol. He straightened out as he grew older and was elected by the tribal council to start a youth center and day care facility. The tribal president at the time, "Cowboy" Fisher, was supportive of an organization for teens, and St. Labre School had donated a building to the tribe for youth work. In 2002, the club raised almost a million dollars in *grants*. Rick and other staff members must constantly write more grant requests to continue the work.

The reservation high school dropout rate is almost 40 percent. That's a

The Northern Cheyenne Boys & Girls Club is a place where struggling teens can find encouragement and help.

> "Elders need to fulfill their calling as cultural teachers by sharing life experiences with the little ones."
>
> —Father Emmett Hoffman

serious problem for the tribe, but Rick says the Boys & Girls Club is a place where kids find "hope instead of hopelessness." It's a place where kids know they have a hot meal, structure, and hugs. For teens, it's a refuge where they won't have to deal with drugs.

The Boys & Girls Club also runs a juvenile diversion program. Teens who get in trouble can go through this program rather than the court system. They must go to drug and alcohol education programs and perform community service.

The club tries to involve youth in as many ways as possible. It even has eight young people who are "junior staff." One high school boy said, "This job is the only reason I've been able to stay sober."

Lame Deer Public High School is another institution that plays a key role in the future of the Northern Cheyenne tribe. When the school opened in 1994, it was long overdue. Way back in 1868, the federal government had promised a school to the Northern Cheyenne, but the promise went unfulfilled for a very long time. By the 1990s, Lame Deer was the largest community in the state of Montana without a public high school—and the Northern Cheyenne Reservation was the only reservation of its size without a high school. The tribal council and Norma Bixby (then head of the tribal education department) worked hard to get the school.

Today the school gives hope to young people like Micaiah Birdinground, a seventeen-year-old senior at Lame Deer High School who is vice president of her class. Micaiah's favorite classes are English and Cheyenne language and culture class. Like many of her peers, she speaks little of her native language—but she enjoyed the class so much she took it twice and would have taken it again if she had been allowed to do so. Students in the class learn their language, do beading, and make *dreamcatchers*.

Micaiah plans to continue her education after high school and become a registered nurse. At the same time, she wants to stay close to her family so she can be near her two-year-old brother, Isaiah. Like all teens, she has a favorite food—*fry bread*, either with honey or made into Indian tacos—and activities she loves—watching basketball games around the reservation with her cousins. She sees alcoholism as the major challenge facing teens on the reservation.

Seventeen-year-old Reasco Killsnight, a junior, is another young person who is benefiting from the Lame Deer High School. Reasco is president of

A powwow dancer's outfit can be an expression of the owner's artistic skill, personality, and spirituality.

The powwow at the National Mall at Washington D.C. in 2002 gave Native people of many nations the opportunity to share their cultures and display their pride at the U.S. Capitol.

the Lame Deer High School Indian Club, which sponsors a ***powwow*** and parade in September. The club also takes part in community service projects.

Reasco's father is a Sun Dancer who worships in traditional ways. Like Micaiah, Reasco enjoys eating fry bread and watching basketball games. He sees the racism outside the reservation as the major challenge for Northern Cheyenne teens today.

An article in the *Billings Gazette* describes an unusual class at Lame Deer High School taught by Steve Brady. Brady thought students should be learning about the Council of Forty-four Chiefs, the Dog Soldiers, the Indian Reorganization Act, and other matters related to Northern Cheyenne civic life. He had one problem, though—no textbook covered these subjects. So Brady learned from tribal elders, studied books, and met with other teachers to create a ***curriculum*** for Northern Cheyenne tribal government class. The class was so successful the school board decided to make it a required course. Lame Deer is now the only reservation high school in Montana that requires students to study tribal government. Students learn about great leaders, sacred sites, treaties, U.S. Indian policies, and their own reservation's tribal government.

IBM and the Montana State University in Bozeman are also doing their part to help high school students at the Northern Cheyenne and other Montana Indian reservations achieve academic success. Each summer, Indian high school students come to the Bozeman campus for six weeks of classes and hands-on laboratory work. Students are excited while together on campus, but unfortunately, once they return to their homes, their academic interest often wanes. Many of them live in geographically isolated homes, and they lack friends who share their interests.

To help this situation, the college asked IBM to provide ThinkPad computers so the students could keep in touch with each other and with the program during the year. Students are required to log in three times a week to the college program site, where they interact with college instructors and other students. If they do that faithfully, the computers are theirs to keep after graduation. Participating students say the computers have helped tremendously—in everything from homework to social life.

Older Northern Cheyenne also have special needs. Chief Charlie Sitting Man Jr. once said: "My people are packed off to towns where they don't

The Crow/Northern Cheyenne Indian Hospital is a 24-bed hospital that opened in 1995 and serves both tribes.

Leroy White Man, Northern Cheyenne artist, leans on a rifle used by his grandfather. Much of Leroy's artwork celebrates the history and customs of his people.

Chapter 6

Contemporary Arts

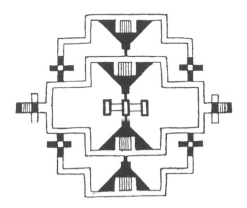

Like many Indians, Leroy White Man does not like to boast about his accomplishments—but he has lived an eventful life. His surname comes from a misunderstanding a long time ago. His grandfather had the given name "Man Who Paints Himself White," referring to the face paint instructions he received in a vision. Later, a non-Indian misheard the name and shortened it to "White Man." Leroy's Indian name is "Ma'eve'ese," which means Red Bird. His father was Black Hawk, descendent of Black Bear, descendent of Ve'heo, who fought Custer's troops at Little Bighorn.

Leroy was born on the Northern Cheyenne Reservation in Lame Deer, Montana. As a child, Leroy made his own toys. Later in his life, this childhood experience developed into his artistic career. Growing up, he spent much time with his mother's side of the family. His mother and grandparents spoke Old Cheyenne and practiced a traditional lifestyle. The traditional Northern Cheyenne ways are an important part of Leroy's life today. He is a member of the Kit Fox society, and a Sun Dance instructor.

As a young man, Leroy was a boxer. In 1960, he won the Wyoming State Golden Glove finals. He joined the Air Force and continued boxing in the armed service, becoming a champion boxer in the USAF European league.

After he finished his service in the armed forces, Leroy spent much of his time with horses. Today, he owns six thousand acres (405 hectares) of range and has a herd of horses. Every year, he provides sixty horses for the reenactment of the Battle of Little Bighorn.

Clearly, Leroy's life has been full of more than just art. Like many artists, he uses the varied experiences of his life for inspiration. His favorite artistic *medium* is stone. He is a take-away sculptor; he starts with a chunk of stone and removes pieces until the sculpture is finished. His second-favorite medium is painting, but whether he paints or sculpts, his art reflects stories told by his grandfather and other tribal elders, along with his own visions and dreams. Although he has had no formal art training, he

Leroy White Man stands by one of his large paintings.

Award-winning sculpture by Leroy White Man.

Leroy White Man carved this eagle out of a piece of elk horn.

received awards in a variety of mediums. Each year, he donates an original painting to be raffled off to raise money for the run commemorating Dull Knife's breakout from Fort Robinson.

Leroy White Man enjoys speaking to school groups. He tells the students stories, and sometimes he reads them a book about horses that he wrote and illustrated for his daughter. He also does "ten-second drawings." Leroy draws these while he faces the audience, talking while he draws upside down on a pad that also faces the audience!

In 2002, Leroy won the Native American Juried Art Show in the bronze division. His winning piece, a sculpture of a bison, is called *The Hunter and the Hunted*. First he carved it from stone, and then he covered it with bronze. Although the Tsetsêhesêstâhase no longer live off the herds, buffalo are still important to traditional Northern Cheyenne today.

Leroy White Man works in a wide variety of mediums. This eagle was created by cutting away fur on a hide.

Some Northern Cheyenne artists continue to work in the artistic traditions of the past. Leroy's daughter Emma White Man, for example, does fine beadwork. Before the white people came, beads were made from animal horns and teeth, pieces of wood, or hard seeds. Flattened porcupine quills were an especially fine form of decoration. The Cheyenne had special women's quillwork societies where beautiful quilled objects would be made as a form of prayer. The quilled pieces themselves were not sacred—but the process of making them was. Owning a beautifully decorated object was not as important as making it in a sacred way.

European traders introduced tiny beads—called seed beads—to the Cheyenne. They are the most popular beads for Northern Cheyenne beadwork today. Indian women invented two techniques for using them: loom beading and appliqué embroidery. Both ways of beading are used today. "Lazy stitch" was a style of beading invented by Plains Indian tribes in the 1800s. A needle is pulled partially through leather, pulled up to the surface, and then beads are strung. Lazy stitch is still used today on beaded Northern Cheyenne moccasins. The beads are made in Czechoslovakia.

The Northern Cheyenne not only excel in the visual arts; today they have a number of outstanding musical artists as well. Native Reign, for instance, is a performance group that combines traditional Cheyenne dances with drama and contemporary music. Their presentations present the history of the Northern Cheyenne people. Native Reign travels and gives performances throughout the western United States and Canada. In 1999,

Joseph Fire Crow is an award-winning Northern Cheyenne flute player.

they received the Governor's Award at the State Capital Building for their music.

Joseph Fire Crow is a Northern Cheyenne musician who has achieved international acclaim for his traditional flute playing. Joseph was born in Montana and raised on the Northern Cheyenne Reservation. Growing up, he enjoyed the outdoors and powwows—but when he was nine years old, he was placed with a foster family in Seattle as part of the Mormon Indian Placement Program. This was a program sponsored by the Latter Day Saints Church, which placed "disadvantaged" Indian children with non-Indian families during the school year. Joseph Fire Crow was happy in his early years, yet according to the program's guidelines, he was considered "disadvantaged." Indians today say the program turned kids into "apples"—red outside and white inside. To a large degree, this was true in Joseph's case; he joined in Mormon worship and attended Brigham Young University in Provo, Utah, as many Mormon young people do.

In his final year at college, Joseph read the book *Cheyenne Memories* by John Stands in Timber; the book helped him reconnect with his heritage. During this process, he met John Rainier of New Mexico, who showed him how to make and play an Indian flute. Joseph left behind Mormon influences and returned to the Northern Cheyenne Reservation. He became respected as a flutist; at first, he played for weddings and funerals on the reservation, but gradually his reputation grew.

Joseph Fire Crow's soothing flute recordings have been described as "a national treasure." His music has been released on CDs for both American and European labels. He also shares his music and tribal history at speaking engagements.

Gary Small is yet another Northern Cheyenne musician. Gary (whose cousin is tribal president Geri Small) was raised in Montana and now lives in Portland, Oregon. He sings and plays blues guitar and also plays *roots rock* and *reggae*. The Gary Small Band is a very talented ensemble. Congo player Bobby Torres played at the first Woodstock concert, and Graham Lear, who also plays with the band, is a former drummer for musician Carlos Santana.

Gary Small talked about his heritage in an interview for PRS Forum:

Non-Indians have an odd concept of who and what Native Americans really are. Your "Indian-ness" has more to do with how you were brought

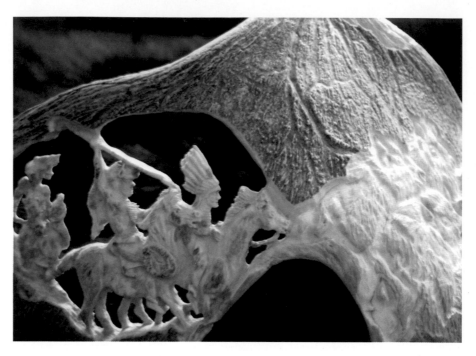

Elk horn carving by Leroy White Man portrays Northern Cheyenne warriors on horseback.

up and if you are part of the Indian community or culture, not whether you are full-blood or half-breed, from this tribe or that, and all that racial [stuff].

He believes music is a way to break down stereotypes and racial walls.

Another boundary-spanning Northern Cheyenne musician is Ed Walks-nice who performs with the group Lunar Drive. Lunar Drive is described as "a fusion of Native American chants and beats, *techno*, *electronica*, *hip-hop* and dance." They have played in England, Australia, and New Zealand.

Ed Walksnice performs **grass dance**, **human beatbox**, and Native American and English vocals. When he was six years old, a white family in Michigan adopted him, but he rediscovered his heritage when he was in his twenties. His musical influences range from the Beatles to powwow dancing. He hopes to "reflect Indian culture through new contexts like techno and hip-hop."

The Northern Cheyenne have a long heritage of creativity. Today they express that same creativity through both the visual and musical arts. Combining traditional Cheyenne techniques with modern influences, the power and beauty of their work is appreciated by both Indians and non-Indians alike.

U.S. Senator Ben Nighthorse Campbell has made many significant contributions to the United States and the rights of Indian nations.

Chapter 7

Contributions to the World

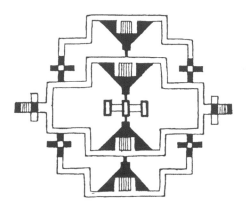

Ben Nighthorse Campbell has made many contributions both to America and to Indians. Currently, he is the senior U.S. senator from Colorado and the only American Indian on the U.S. Senate.

A member of the Northern Cheyenne tribe, Ben Nighthorse Campbell has had a very exciting life. He was born in 1933 in Auburn, California; his mother, Mary Vierra, was a Portuguese immigrant, and his father, Albert Campbell, was a Northern Cheyenne Indian. Ben's early years were hard, since his mother was frequently hospitalized with *tuberculosis* and his father drank heavily. By the time he was ten, Nighthorse had spent half his life in an orphanage. During the time he spent with his parents, he and his sister were often neglected. As he grew older, he gravitated toward other troubled teens in the streets.

Powwows are an opportunity for Native people young and old to show pride in their heritage.

Chapter 8

Challenges for Today, Hopes for the Future

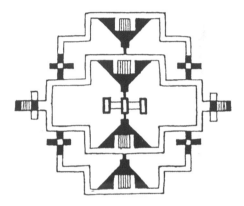

"The Northern Cheyenne Tribe has many needs. The tribal council and tribal administration try to address these needs on a daily basis. However, we are overwhelmed and often feel like we are trying to put out a forest fire with a garden hose."

Tribal president Geri Small spoke these words in 2001 to the U.S. Senate Committee on Indian Affairs. No wonder she felt so overwhelmed! The Northern Cheyenne face many challenges.

Economic needs are significant on the reservation. As President Small pointed out, "The unemployment rate on our reservation is at constant 65 percent." One way the tribe has worked at improving the economy is by working with local banks.

In the early 1980s, Gail Small and her group, Native Action, challenged the practices of First Interstate Bank. She claimed the bank was profiting from Northern Cheyenne transactions, yet making few loans to tribal members. After thirteen years of dialogue, the bank opened an office in Lame Deer on the reservation. Gail Small reports, "We've seen a huge increase of lending on the reservation. I think overall it was one of the key ingredients to helping economic development here."

Despite such economic gains, there are still few jobs on the Northern Cheyenne Reservation. Tribal government and Bureau of Indian Affairs offices are the largest employers. St. Labre and other schools and a few locally owned businesses also provide some employment. Fire fighting provides jobs for adults, teens, and sometimes for entire families. The recent coal development hiring agreement should help provide jobs in the next few years.

In 2002, the new Charging Horse Casino opened. The casino is a 1.4 million-dollar gaming facility that replaced a very small gaming facility on the same site, a stone's throw from Head Chief and Young Mule Memorial Hill, where a century ago two young Northern Cheyenne men made a

The new Charging Horse Casino is located next to Head Chief and Young Mule Memorial Hill, where a century ago two young Northern Cheyenne charged a troop of armed soldiers.

At the rate the Northern Cheyenne tribe is presently funded, it will take 35 years for every family on the reservation to have its own home.

suicide dash toward a row of armed soldiers. Gaming has been helpful for the Northern Cheyenne, though their remote location means they cannot make tremendous amounts of money from the business since few people are willing to travel so far.

Housing is also a challenge on the Northern Cheyenne Reservation. President Geri Small's report to the government states: "The tribe has over 700 families waiting for a home on the Northern Cheyenne Reservation. At the rate the tribe is presently funded, it will take thirty-five years to provide these families a home." Many existing homes are poorly constructed.

Faced with all these problems, some people turn to drugs and alcohol to escape from their unhappiness. The Northern Cheyenne Nation is a "dry" reservation, which means alcohol is illegal there, but people can buy alcohol at nearby towns. Between 1991 and 1996, twelve people died in alcohol-related auto accidents on the reservation. During the same years, 125 child abuse cases were related to drinking. Alcohol can also cause deaths by suicides, accidents, or alcohol poisoning. The tribe has no facility for alcoholism recovery. People who need medical help getting off alcohol are sometimes just given medication and sent home from local health care facilities.

Methamphetamines or "crank" is another addictive drug found on the Northern Cheyenne Reservation. One young Cheyenne mother, who almost lost her son because of crank, says: "You lose everything, your self-respect, family, friends, and it's not worth it!"

Health issues on the Northern Cheyenne Reservation are also serious. Tribal President Geri Small reported to the Senate committee: "Diabetes is devastating our tribal population." Eighty-six percent of the children on the reservation are at risk for diabetes; 443 people on the reservation already have the disease. *Dialysis* treatment is not available on the reservation, so tribal members must drive for hours to be treated.

Diabetes may be *genetically* caused, but it can also be caused by high-fat diets and little exercise. Traditional Northern Cheyenne lifeways were very healthy, but now many people on the reservation have become ill due to the unhealthy patterns of non-Indian culture.

The health of the land, as well as that of the people, is a great concern for the future of the Northern Cheyenne. The state is pushing coal bed methane development all around the Northern Cheyenne Nation. Ground-water and surface water on the reservation may be affected.

Coal mining presents a difficult challenge to the Northern Cheyenne. On the one hand, the mines may offer badly needed jobs. On the other hand, Grandmother Earth will suffer—along with the people who depend on her. Tribal leaders must wage a nonstop battle to try and keep jobs while avoiding environmental damage.

With all these threats, many Northern Cheyenne feel the greatest threat is the loss of their language. Cultural identity and sacred beliefs, which give self-esteem and unique identity to the tribe, will be lost if the language is forgotten. Conrad Fisher, Dean of Cultural Affairs at Chief Dull Knife College, says that passing down the culture was easier in the older days. Families would gather together by fireplaces and listen to their elders. Now, many children have televisions in their own rooms, both parents work outside the home, and children spend more time with their peers.

Recently, a survey taken on the reservation indicated that 28 percent of the Northern Cheyenne spoke their language fluently, while 22 percent could speak it only poorly. In the 1970s, it was not fashionable to speak

Institutions like Head Start, the Boys & Girls Club, and the public schools play an increasingly important role in the success and cultural vitality of Northern Cheyenne children.

Cheyenne. Now, the people realize the essential role language plays in keeping their culture.

The battle to teach Cheyenne language is now being fought in public institutions as much as in families. Public schools serving the reservation offer Cheyenne language classes for fifty minutes, three times a week. The Head Start program on the reservation teaches language to little ones (see chapter five). St. Labre teaches Northern Cheyenne language and culture. Chief Dull Knife College emphasizes traditional language and culture.

Although family traditions have been weakened, Northern Cheyenne ways are still being passed down from generation to generation. In 1999,

St. Labre School provides education for more than 700 Northern Cheyenne and Crow children, and provides employment for many tribal members.

for example, Leroy White Man drove one of his grandsons, who was then ten, to the gateway of Yellowstone Park. A group of Indians from various tribes had walked five hundred miles to this place over twenty days to protest the killing of buffalo that wander out of the park. Leroy remembers: "On the windswept, muddy field, the Indian people prayed, sang, and listened to the leaders from many tribes."

The event ended with a piercing ritual, which had not been done outside a reservation for more than a century. Joseph Chasing Horse, a Lakota spiritual leader, explained: "Long ago, the buffalo gave his blood for us.

Today, we give our blood for him." Gary Silk, a Lakota, had two sharp sticks stuck through his shoulders. Ropes, tied to buffalo skulls, were attached to these. He danced four times in a circle, honoring the four sacred directions. Then Silk grabbed hold of a horse, and the sticks were torn out of his back.

Despite getting up at five in the morning, driving half a day, and standing in a cold wet field, Leroy's grandson never once complained about hunger or cold. He was quiet for a while in the car driving back, and Leroy thought the boy was asleep. Then the boy spoke into the silence: "Grandpa, AWESOME!"

Leroy White Man says, "I have a very good feeling that I have someone who feels the way I do and will follow the Indian ways."

The Northern Cheyenne today face challenges of poverty and threats to their cultural identity. Tribal politicians, activists, teachers, business peo-

The Cheyenne people follow an ancient roadway that connects centuries of tradition with the twenty-first century.

Biographies

Kenneth McIntosh is a pastor and his wife, Marsha, is a schoolteacher. They both took leave from their regular jobs to work on this series. Formerly, Kenneth worked as a junior high teacher in Los Angeles, California. He wrote *Clergy* for the Mason Crest series "Careers with Character." The McIntoshes live in upstate New York and have two children, Jonathan and Eirené. They are grateful for the opportunity this work has given them to travel and meet with many wonderful Native people.

Martha McCollough received her bachelor's and master's degrees in anthropology at the University of Alaska-Fairbanks, and she now teaches at the University of Nebraska. Her areas of study are contemporary Native American issues, ethnohistory, and the political and economic issues that surround encounters between North American Indians and Euroamericans.

Benjamin Stewart, a graduate of Alfred University, is a freelance photographer and graphic artist. He traveled across North America to take the photographs included in this series.